SMART CAREER PLANNER

DR DHEERAJ MEHROTRA

XpressPublishing
An imprint of Notion Press

No.8, 3rd Cross Street,CIT Colony,
Mylapore, Chennai, Tamil Nadu-600004

ISBN 978-1-63669-340-8

This book is dedicated to all the wonderful kids who are into the process of making their career ahead. It marvels their efforts and commitment.

Contents

Foreword

The book is a purposeful notion towards the planning of a career. The guidelines suggested in the book laminate success in the long run.

Preface

Friends, Choosing a career is an art and a science. It involves both the mechanism of research and modeling in particular.

The activated strategies discussed within the book reflect ideas on selecting the future in action.

The book SMART CAREER PLANNER is a routine towards being street smart towards choosing a career. It reflects at ease and perfection the ideas and guidelines on selecting and exploring the preparedness for the chosen career in totality.

As a guide, a ready reckoner and a reference, the book targets a showcase on strategies and progressive win-win approaches towards choosing a career.

I invite more queries via tqmhead@aol.com

Dr Dheeraj Mehrotra

www.authordheerajmehrotra.com

Acknowledgements

I acknowledge with thanks the wonderful network of educators/ students/ parents I am engaged with around the globe.

My thanks to their fellowship and salutations for the best wishes as always.

I am also thankful to over 1,16,000 followers at www.facebook.com/rockstarteachers who believe and trust me on my notion.

Thank You All!

ONE
SMART CAREER PLANNING

TIP #1

Look into yourself what you are good at.
Prepare yourself to learn: In order to learn, you need to be prepared for learning. Without preparations, you cannot learn. If you fail to PLAN you PLAN to fail.

TIP #2

Think of jobs you can do that allow you to do what you are good at. Gather the resources for learning: Learning involves reading, writing, listening, watching, and practicing. You need to have books, notebooks, videos, podcasts and webcasting. Cash on WWW- Whatever, Whenever, Wherever learning policy.

TIP #3

Shake off your anxiety and stress. Do some INFORMATION INTERVIEWING. If your mind is anxious and stressful, you cannot learn. You can learn well only when your mind is at peace. Have joy while Learning. Information Interviewing can be done with informal discussions with the industry employees or professionals of the field which interests you.

TIP #4

Explore the NETWORKING sites like LINKED IN to know more about the profession you are opting to choose. Get to the user groups and set the platform for yourself. It allows a great way to reach people in a specific industry.

TIP #5

Set a balanced approach for better learning: Select the kind of work which you seem to enjoy. Aim at a profession which inspires you to want a become excellent in the field. Selecting your major definite purpose in life is the starting point of your personal greatness.

TIP #6

Boost your mental capacity: In order to learn, your brain should function properly. Your brain will function better if you use it more. You have to use your brain to think, to contemplate and to analyze. Make sure you Opt for the option with no fear and pressure. Get some advice.

TIP #7

Take a brain supplement: You can boost your brain by taking brain supplements or foods that enhance the memory. Teachers often suggest **DARK CHOCOLATES**for better memory! Just chase out your biggest fear about choosing a career path. Make a balance between academics and extra curricular activities.

TIP #8

Sleep well for better learning: There has been numerous research on how a good sleep helps in better understanding and analytical thinking. Sleep for 8 hours, work for 8 hours but not the same 8 hours! Make sure you determine if you want a JOB , Career or Calling!

TIP #9

Develop deep concentration: You need to concentrate on lessons to learn it. Without concentration, you cannot learn. Explore learning by understanding the content as a story. Make use of ICT – the videos to explore the learning topic wise. Taste wise and get the best about the plan of career you have.

TIP #10

Take a break to learn better: Taking a break from your everyday life boosts your creativity and mental capacity. Long study hours will not help you in learning. Make sure you decide on what type of a role is work going to play in your life story? Act and decide. Avoid glamour driven extra curricular activities.

TIP #11

Declare your interest on JOB, as a supporting role, Career as the lead role and Calling as the whole movie. Frame the direction with YOU in mind not the CANDIDATE or the REFERENCE you receive from your nears and dears.

TIP #12

Change your focus: Studying the same subject again and again will only create monotony. In order to break that monotony, you need to change your subject quite often, for instance, you can switch between science and arts. Ask yourself the question: When and where can I make money to pursue my dreams?

TIP #13

Reading: Reading is the most common method to learn. If you want to learn something, you have to read about it. Browse the NET, read newspapers or a post of social networking. News on apps is not exceptional even. Read about the plans/ actions. Something that stimulates you on a daily basis. Read about when you think about work in the larger scare of your life.

TIP #14

Rereading: One-time reading may not help you understand everything, for better understanding, you have to reread. The second reading will give you a better TIP, even more, the third reading. This applies to your notes and chapters. Explore the things that defines you and the impact you want to have on the world.

TIP #15

How do you see your work in future? Check on your passion in life. Define yourself on the calling and which one is right for you? Check your happiness quotient for the future work and calling. De

TIP #16

Analytical thinking: In order to learn something, you need to have analytical thinking. Analytical thinking means you analyze the TIP carefully. Make sure you honour the past and energise the future.

TIP #17

Learning by listening: Listen to your elders/ teachers/ parents about a Career Option looking at your strengths and weakness. Get Rid of your jealousy about career options and people who carry them. Believe in your strengths and multiply them towards choosing a career.

TIP #18

Learning from the environment: The environment is a great teacher. You can learn so many things from the surrounding. Check what you are afraid of? Give a reminder to your potentials and work on your weakness to cater to the needs.

TIP #19

Developing interest: You won't learn anything until you are interested in it. For instance, if you are not interested in math, you will never learn math. Turn your jealousy into admiration. Find ways to move positively toward your goals.

TIP #20

Exploration: If you want to learn, you have to explore. Exploring means examining something, analyzing it thoroughly. Reach out to your career guides/ teachers for help and support. Gaze information on priority. Work on your skills.

TIP #21

Research: Researching is a great way to learn. When you research about something, you will know about it.

Practice CURATING knowledge. Identify possible career directions. Have and OPTION B. Look at the things that bug you. Frustrations, things that angry you, things you want to see improved. Anything like that would be a possible career direction for you in the long run.

TIP #22

Work on the problems you care about. Match with your skill set and create an option for your career. Big or small, what thing would you like to see improved. Your hobbies and interests. Brainstorm over it and work out as a case study for selection a career option for your good self.

TIP #23

Learning from young ones: People younger than you can also teach you so many things because every person is special and he/she is intelligent in his/her own ways. Check on the problems do you what to solve. This would give you a spectrum towards your choosing a career option.

TIP #24

Classroom learning: Classroom learning refers to attending school, college and training centers for formal education. Formal education is the most popular learning method. You always need a facilitator to learn and explore knowledge. Try taking the maximum through queries. This by large helps you in knowing and figuring about the options for career you would prefer.

TIP #25

Distance learning: You can get a formal information about a career or an option to explore via: **UDEMY, COURSERA, LYNDA, EDX**and others of choice. Get set go. Grab the opportunity and master with time. Use Personas to narrow down your career direction.

TIP #26

Map your ideas, flow diagrams and make some sticky notes about the options you are looking it. It shall help you to steer in the long run with a valid career option.

TIP #27

Learning from the real world: The real word is the best classroom to learn various things. In order to learn from the real world, you have to be a keen observer. Tabulate your likes and dislikes and develop your interest towards excellence.

TIP #28

Study: In order to learn, you have to study. Studying does not only mean virtual/real classroom studying, studying also refers to learning by self-study. Always keep and refer to some books apart from your TEXT or prescribed books.

TIP #29

Smart learning: In order to lean, you need to study. However, you should also have a right approach to studying. You need to acquire smart studying techniques. Learn to browse smart. Blog your queries and showcase your social presence via putting queries.

TIP #30

Online discussion boards: Online discussion boards and online forums can provide a good platform to build up knowledge and skills. Get going with your ONLINE REPUTATION MANAGEMENT by posting and hosting knowledge of your interest.

TIP #31

Blogs and websites: Blogs and websites provide a great resource for learning various things, from simple things such as writing an essay to complicated things such a web programming.

TIP #32

Online search: Search engines like Google can help you research on any topics and provide you resources on anything you want to learn. Make use of some more search engines and be an innovator and a contributor to learning through contribution to Wikipedia!

TIP #33

Learning from videos: Seeing is believing, therefore, you will learn better from instructional and educative videos than from a classroom lecture. Upload your own youtube videos, vimeos' and even comment on the ones you watch and share!

TIP #34

Learning from audio media: Technology has created audio books, now you don't have to read books to learn, you can listen to books. Audiobooks and podcasts are great tools for learning.

TIP #35

Learning from Peers. Take the best from your friends, colleagues, relatives and teachers. Share and explore the learning to the best of use and meaning.

TIP #36

Social Media: You might be using social media for fun, but have you realized the potential of social media in learning? Get a page made of topic of your choice and explore learning through share and re-posting.

TIP #37

Group collaboration: Form small groups of learners and give them something to contemplate. Shuffle the group members and let them discuss the same TIP. Use brainstorming to generate TIPs and share knowledge.

TIP #38

Question and Answer sites: Ask, Yahoo answers, Quora are some of the questions and answer sites that can answer your questions. These are the best means to get known to the unknown facts.

TIP #39

Using iTunesU for learning: iTunesU is an Apple platform for the distribution of podcasts, videos, apps, and other digital media in various categories. These media are great learning tools. Explore the LINKEDIN learning modules.

TIP #40

Smartphone Apps: On Google Play and Apple store you can find many learning apps. You can find these learning apps for free or by paying little money. Some of them include: Pathsource, Good&Co, Eventbrite, CamCard.

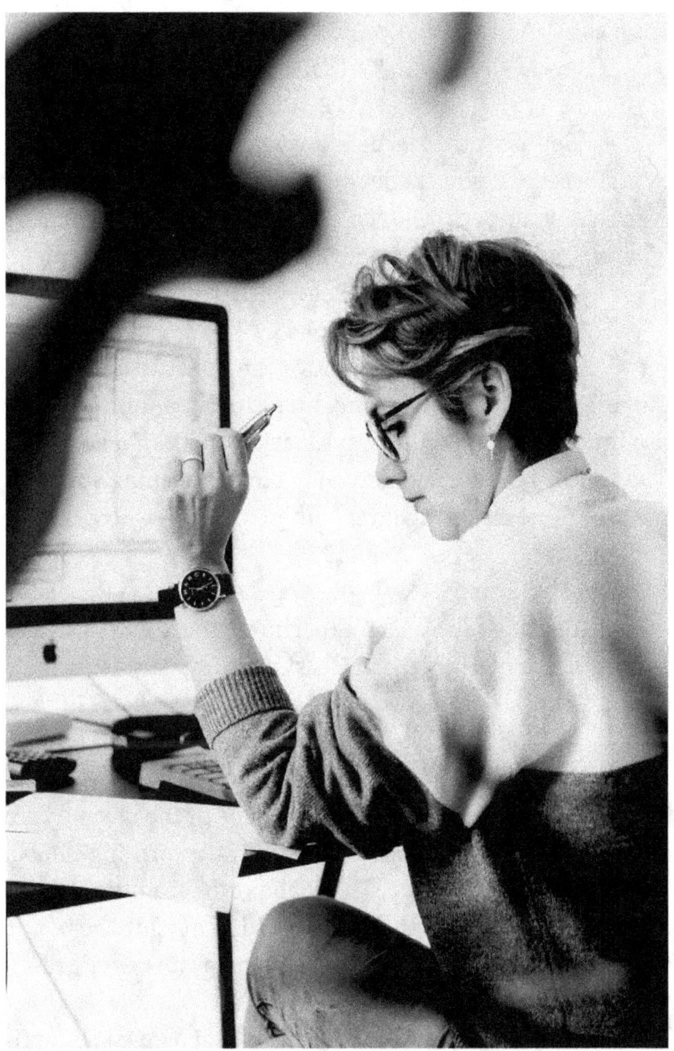

TIP #41

Active learning: Active learning means the learners are involved with interactive problem solving by sharing TIPs and skills. Add skills to your profile via apps like UDEMY, UDACITY, DUOLONGO.

TIP #42

Self-directed learning: By evaluating your own performance, you can learn so many things. When you analyze your performance, you will know your strength and weakness. Get Set go with the inspiration and the confidence to get ahead with the career.

TIP #43

Innovative learning: Innovation refers to creating something new through study and experimentation. If you are innovative, you will always learn something new. Select for the best avenue for you to choose keeping your strengths and the interest in view.

TIP #44

Learning through a role-playing: Role playing will teach you through self-direction, experimentation, and practice. Interact or observe the professionals of your taste and hunger. It should fuel your passion and a purpose in the long run with the desired selection.

TIP #45

Brainstorming: Brainstorming is one of the best ways to develop an TIP or elaborate the TIP. Brainstorming can be done singly or in a group. Think about the traditional roles that are available but also try to think outside the box towards selection of a career which has just emerged.

TIP #46

Interactive learning: Learners can get engaged with the interactive learning by participating in question and answer sessions. It is through this and with full intention that you do a selection and things fall into place. A positive direction and an attitude comes all together.

TIP #47

Learning through trial and error: If you don't try, you will not learn. In order to learn something, you should never be afraid of mistakes that you are going to make. Assess Yourself with enough thought into it and you shall increase your chance of making a good decision about a career option.

TIP #48

Practice makes you perfect: If you don't practice, you will never learn. Practice means you do it again and again. Make a list of occupations or professions to explore. Match them with your choice and priorities. Make a career action plan.

TIP #49

Learning by memorizing: Memorizing means repeating something in your mind again and again, and recording in your mind so that you can recall it when you need it. Visit various blogs and sites of Universities/ Colleges. Research on the occupations that appeal to you the most.

TIP #50

Learning from storyboard: Storyboard is a great method of learning lessons that requires memorization and visual interpretations. Storyboard uses infographics, images, and stories. Identify and develop your abilities and interests. It shall help to understand your strengths and limitation to make realistic career choices.

TIP #51

Learning from stories: If the lessons are introduced as stories, learning will not only be fun but also effective. Storytelling technique can be used for children as well as adults. Orient yourself about the importance of self understanding, self accepting and self directing.

TIP #52

Learning through stimulation: Stimulation refers to an act of arousing people to perform an action. By stimulating the learners' mind, it will be easier to impart knowledge. It must involve creating confidence by setting and achieving a goal and to improve job prospects and employability skills.

TIP #53

Welcome new TIPs: In order to lean, your mind must be open to new TIPs. With a closed mind, you will never learn new things. Have a patient listening skill on selecting a career.

TIP #54

Learning from your hobbies: Your hobbies can also help you learn. Think about what your interests are, and then explore your interests. Remember to know yourself with reference to Values, Interests, Strengths, Traits and Ambitions.

TIP #55

Learning by solving puzzles and word games: By solving puzzles you are always learning something new, it can be a new word or new information. Pick up the right career through the smartness through puzzling. Envision yourself as the one you want to do. VISUALIZE yourself with the success you want to robe into....

TIP #56

Board games: Board games are not only fun but also helps in analytical thinking. You can play chess not just for fun but also develop strategies. Help yourself craft a career through grooming. Believe in trying NEW options and things. You can't play a basket ball if you are 5 feet....remember your strengths and weakness.

TIP #57

Go by your traits. Select the OPTION which suits your Intelligence, Capability, Capacity and Priorities in life. Do what you love. You have to get the money thing out of it first. Your career must aim at PROFIT in the long run.

TIP #58

Check if you are WORD SMART and you are strong in reading, writing, telling stories, memorizing dates, thinking in words the possible careers include: Lawyer, Editor, Interpreter/ translator, journalist, playwright, poet, public relations, reporter, teacher, historian, librarian.

TIP #59

Book clubs: By joining a book club, a learner will be introduced to the vast knowledge contained I the books. Book clubs also provide a platform for mutual exchange of TIPs and expressions. This helps exploring career options....and all about them.

TIP #60

Do what you want to do: You will learn only when you love it, if you don't love science, you will never learn anything about science. In order to learn, you have to love it. When you love the subject, you become more creative. Find your purpose, profit and passion and DECIDE a career as an ideal career.

TIP #61

Check if you are NUMBER Smart and you are strong Math, reasoning, logic, problem solving, the possible careers include: Accountant, Analyst, Investment Broker, Lawyer, Chemist, Pharmacist, Physician, Computer Programmer, Engineer, Inventor, Researcher, City Planner.

TIP #62

Learning from newspapers and magazines: Newspapers and magazines are the sources of news, information, and knowledge. Get set go to browse the NEWSPAPERS physically, Read the editorials and get set go.......to decide your Career.

TIP #63

Learning from the radio: Because of its reach and flexibility in using, radio is a great source of learning. You learn a great deal by listening to informative and educative radio programs. Be on the go or learning about options and tasks on the air.....

TIP #64

Learning from TV: TV is a popular medium of entertainment for the people of all ages, however, you should also realize the learning potential of TV. Get to see the positive side and grade the stuff with your prospective career.

TIP #65

Check if you are PICTURE SMART and you are strong in Reading, Maps, Charts, Drawing Mazes, Puzzles, Imagining things the possible careers include: Photographer, Graphic designer, advertiser, architect, artist, carpenter, cartographer, dentist, engineer, interior, designer, mechanic, navigator, pilot, sailor.

TIP #66

Check if you are Body SMART and you are strong in Athletics, dancing, acting, crafts, using tools, the possible careers include: Dancer, coach, athlete, actor/ actress, equestrian, carpenter, massage therapist, magician, mechanic, physical therapist, physician, architect.

TIP #67

Learning through the survey: Survey not only gathers information from the participants but also helps in drawing a conclusion. Mark a survey for the career you need to adopt. It gives you confidence and greets you with the outcome.

TIP #68

Watching documentaries: Documentaries are audio-visual presentations of facts and events. Documentary helps in better understanding. Watch for Shows online of various professionals, TED talks, Youtube Videos and NETFLIX Shows. They provide a ready recknoner of various professions at place.

TIP #69

Check if you are MUSIC SMART and you are strong in Singing/ playing an instrument, picking up sounds, remembering melodies, rhythms, the possible careers include: Conductor, Composer, music teacher, recording technician, singer, sound engineer, musical performer, music critic.

TIP #70

Going to the exhibitions: Exhibitions are open classrooms to learn so many things. By visiting an art exhibition, you will learn about art, by visiting a photography exhibition, you will learn about photography. Similar is the case of the topics which route you to your passion and interest may applicate the encapsulation of a career for your goodself.

TIP #71

Check if you are People Smart and you are strong in Understanding people, leading, organizing, communicating, resolving conflicts, selling, the possible careers include: Teacher, Therapist, Travel Agent, Child Care Worker, Coach, Manager, Mediator, Nurse, Physician, Public Relations, Sales Person

TIP #72

Check if you are Self Smart and you are strong in Understanding self, recognizing strengths and weaknesses, setting goals, the possible careers include: Entrepreneur, Consultant, Counselor, Psychologist or psychiatrist, researcher, writer, trainer.

TIP #73

Change your learning methods: If one learning method is not working for you, change it. For example, if you are unable to grasp from books, watch educational videos. This would help you craft a better CAREER option for you.

TIP #74

Check if you are NATURE SMART and you are strong in Understanding Self, Recognizing strengths and weaknesses, setting goals, Identifying flora and fauna the possible careers include: Botanist, Chef, Environmentalist, landscape artist, navigator, sailor, veterinarian, astronomer, meteorologist, zoologist.

TIP #75

Lose yourself: If you are uptight, you will never have a better understanding of the subject matter. Don't take learning as a burden. Explore the options before you decide on your career path in action.

TIP #76

Recall to understand better: In order to grasp the lesson, you must be able to recall it. You can unable to recall means you did not understand properly. Attend career fairs and seminars. Take things seriously and work on the talk.

TIP #77

Take part in Career Quiz, Career Conferences, Career Fair, Career Tours/ Field Trips, Job Shadowing, Project Work, Role Play, Internship, Mentoring Programmes, Simulation, Career Speeches Competitions.

TIP #78

A picture worth thousand words: A picture has so many things to tell, if you can associate a picture with something, it will be easier to learn. Learn about various options and watch videos about careers in various fields. Visit websites of good institutes, have a webinar with professors/ lecturers of reputed colleges.

TIP #79

Learning through brain map: Brain map is a way to get an overview of something. Brain mapping will help you to see the connections between different TIPs and utilize brainstorming techniques. Make a brain map to explore possibilities of various careers in point of interest.

TIP #80

Go through Journals on Guidance and Counselling, International Journal for Educational and Vocational Guidance, Journal of Career Assessment, Journal of Career Development, Journal of Higher Education, Journal of Vocational Education and Training, The Career Development Quarterly.

TIP #81
Refer to the important career websites viz.
careerbuilder.co.in, archive.india.gov.in, mapmytalent.in,
shiksha.com, careerguidanceindia.com, sarvgyan.com,
dget.nic.in, ugc.ac.in, upsc.gov.in, ncert.nic.in, icda.in
TIP #82
Get inspiration: Inspiration invokes your creativity.
Inspiration invokes your efficiency. You need the
inspiration to become a better at learning something.
Follow the people you admire over TWITTER and other
related platforms. Aim to your role model. The career
advice shall follow.
TIP #83
Develop optimism: Optimism matters in life, even more
in learning. Optimism will help you get involved in
learning. You are a better learner if you are an optimist.
Make a checklist:::POSITIVE ME- What are my values?

What are my skills and abilities? What are my interests? What is my personality Style? What other life goals are important alongwith my job?

TIP #84

State of happiness helps in learning: If you are a happy person, you excel in learning. A sad person or a pessimist individual will always fail in learning. Read Career Guides/ Occupational Monographs/ Occupational Briefs/ Handbooks/ Dictionaries of occupations and Industries/ Career Fictions/ Biographies/ Employment Reviews.

TIP #85

Know what to consider while choosing a college. The priorities include- Accreditation of an Institution, UGC for Higher Education, AICTE for Technical Education, NCTE for Teacher Education, MCI for Medical Education. Suggested Websites: naac.gov.in, aiuweb.org, ugc.ac.in

TIP #86

Learn super learning methods: Scientists and educationists have developed super learning methods. Research on these super learning methods and use the one that is most appropriate for you. A research on CAREER helps you know more about the JOY of adopting.

TIP #87

Know about the COURSE AFFILIATION AND ACCREDITATION, even though the universities are recognized by UGC, it is not necessary that its courses must also be recognized. So while deciding upon joining a course in a University, accreditation of the course has to be ensure.

TIP #88

Consider INTERNSHIPS and HANDS on opportunities with strong connection with the companies and organisations where the students can go for internship.

Always visit the websites and search for the validity and the practice. Reach out to the ALUMNI and decide the career move accordingly.

TIP #89

Set a goal: Having a goal helps you learn better. You should have answers to the question like "what do want to achieve through learning?" Seek the advice, explore the job placement rates of the career you are meeting at.

TIP #90

you should learn in order to make life better. Therefore every learner needs to exercise self-control. Be on the dose of learning and knowing new career options and the universities offering them with pay packages and joy of working.

TIP #91

Learn how to learn as a LIFE SKILL: One of the best ways to learn is learning how to learn. Find out various learning methods and apply the method that best suits you. **Learn what you know and what you don't:**No one is dumb. You know many things that others don't know. To learn something you should know what you already know. You can always learn what you don't know. You do not know that may be your career ahead!

TIP #92

Go beyond the curriculum: It is true that a school/ college goer should excel in the school curriculum, however, there are many things to learn from the real world. This explores options for CAREER moves in the right direction.

TIP #93

Learn from the real-life experience: Classroom learning is important, however, the knowledge you gather from a classroom is never enough in life. You should learn from the real-life experience. Believe in EXPERIENTIAL LEARNING as a delightful affair. Make a choice of the CAREER on the move.

TIP #94

Teach yourself: You should never depend on instructors and teachers to learn. By teaching yourself, you will be equipped with basic knowledge that helps in the learning process. Seek to find the key concept: When you are learning a certain subject, try to find out the key concepts. Once you know what the subject is all about, you will develop the ability to improve your understanding.

TIP #95

Start blogging: Now this might surprise you. However, if you create a blog and publish what you have learned, it will not only help you understand the concepts better but also help other people learn from what you have learned.

TIP #96

Persistence: Thomas Edison once said, "Genius is 1% inspiration and 99% perspiration". Never give up on learning. Don't be intimidated. **Get the experience, not just the course: learning is not all about knowing the concept. Learning is about knowing how to benefit from what you have learned. At the end of the day, the learner should get the experience, not just the course.**

TIP #97

Challenge yourself: Generally speaking, you are more intelligent than you realize. Attempt to do something you have never done, you will realize your true potential.

TIP #98

Don't be afraid of castigation: The world is full of cynics. There are people around us who always try to downgrade us. Don't be afraid of people who criticize you.

TIP #99

Don't be afraid of failures: It is not possible to succeed in every walk of life. Failures are the part of our life. Find a mentor: If you have a mentor, it is easier to get to the next level quickly. A mentor will offer you valuable perspective and experience that will improve your skills and knowledge.

TIP #100

Learning from workshops: Workshop is a brief intensive course for a small group of learners that emphasize on problem-solving. In addition, Gather and assess information: If you are learning something, gather as much information as you can, and then analyze the information and interpret insightfully.

The Street Smart Learning on the go!Available at
www.amazon.in

About The Author

www.dheerajmehrotra.com

Dheeraj Mehrotra, a white and a yellow belt in SIX SIGMA, a Certified NLP Business Diploma holder, is an Educational Innovator, Author, with expertise in Six Sigma In Education, Academic Audits, Neuro Linguistic Programming (NLP), Total Quality Management In Education, an Experiential Educator, a CBSE Resource towards School Assessment (SQAA), CCE, JIT, Five S and KAIZEN. He has authored over **40**books on Computer Science for ICSE/ ISC/ CBSE Students, over **10** books of academic interest for the field of education excellence and Six Sigma. A former Principal at De Indian Public School, New Delhi, (INDIA) with an ample teaching experience of over Two Decades, he is a certified Trainer for Quality Circles/ TQM in Education and QCI Standards for School Accreditation/ Six Sigma in Education. He has also been honored with the **President of India'sNational Teacher Award in the year 2006** and the**Best Science Teacher State Award** (By the Ministry of Science and Technology, State of UP), **Innovation in Education**for his inception of Six Sigma In Education by Education Watch, New Delhi and **Education World- Best Teacher Award**, BOLT Learner Teacher Award by Air India, **'Innovation in Education Award 2016'** by Higher Education Forum (HEF), Gujarat Chapter, among others. He has developed over **150 FREE EDUCATIONAL MOBILE Apps**for the Google Play Store exclusively for Teachers, Students and Parents. This work has been recognized by the **LIMCA BOOK OF RECORDS & INDIA BOOK OF RECORDS**as the only Indian to draw that feast. Dr. Mehrotra is presently working as an **Academic Evangelist**in India. He has conducted over 1000 workshops globally on "Excellence In Education" integrated with Total Quality Management and Six Sigma, Technology Integration in Education (TIE), Developing towards being

ROCKSTAR TEACHERS, including Cyberspace, Cyber Security, Classroom Management, School Leadership & Management and Innovative teaching within classrooms via Mind Maps, NLP and Experiential Learning in Academics. As a UDEMY Premium Instructor, he has over 300 Online Courses with around 7 Lakh enrollments from 180 plus nations around the world. He can be visited at www.authordheerajmehrotra.com

www.ingramcontent.com/pod-product-compliance
Lightning Source LLC
Chambersburg PA
CBHW070225260726
48658CB00006BA/2181